Urho A. Pietilä

Suomi
FINLAND

Finns are the result of their own and many other peoples' imagination.
A specific wisdom as regards their past and a special vision of their future are characteristic of the Finn. As the past is continuously expanding and the amount of future inexhaustible, Finns are becoming wiser and wiser everyday.

Tacitus

Designer: Urho A. Pietilä
Art director: Kirsti Pietilä
Captions: Pauli Pyykölä and Heikki J. Hakala
Translator: Paul Westlake

The book was published simultaneously in Finnish.

Printed in Finland 1996 by T-Print Ky

ISBN 951-31-0767-1

FINLAND
Suomi

Photographs by Urho A. Pietilä

Text by Heikki J. Hakala

KUSTANNUSOSAKEYHTIÖ TAMMI
HELSINKI

Those who enter Finland by sea are treated to a heartfelt
welcome from the heart of the capital. The Finnish way
of life is accentuated in the city´s most famous
marketplace, located opposite the presidential palace.

A people far away from each other

Finland is a European state and the easternmost of the five Nordic countries. The country occupies 338,000 square kilometres, making it the seventh biggest country on its continent, including Russia and its Asian territories. It's slightly smaller than Germany and a little larger than its neighbour, Norway.

Although there's plenty of space, there aren't that many people – only 15 inhabitants per square kilometre, making a total of 5.1 million. In a European context such numbers are modest, but in terms of its northern location, between the 60th and 70th parallel, they're quite remarkable. The Arctic Circle cuts across the north of the country, capturing a quarter of its land area.

Finns decided to populate their country very unevenly. Altogether, Finland has twelwe counties but the majority of the population live in the three south-westernmost provinces. The further north you go the less populated the country becomes, with Lapland boasting as few as two inhabitants per square kilometre. More than half of Finland's population live in a little over a hundred towns. The concept of a town is a very flexible one in Finland and even its cities are small. The capital, Helsinki, has just over half a million inhabitants. And Kaskinen, for example, which was officially recognized as a town two hundred years ago, only has about 1,500 inhabitants.

The other half of the population still dwell in the countryside and many of them live far away from each other, well out of view of a neighbour. But even in the country, more and more people have been moving to villages and built-up areas. Finns have inherited a longing for privacy, peace and quiet from their ancestors who built their early homesteads deep in the woods. Although changing times have driven Finns closer to one another, social interaction is not as vibrant as it is in more southern countries.

Finland's two official languages are Finnish and Swedish and, in some Lapp municipalities, Lapp. Swedish was for long the language of the ruling classes as well as of those that resided in coastal areas. But as time went by Finnish gradually became the predominant language. In consequence, the significance of Swedish diminished and nowadays a mere six per cent of the population speak Swedish as their mother tongue. Nevertheless, it's still regarded as an indication of Finland's pluralism and cultural richness. There have, however, also been many disputes over language. Discussion was heated in the 1900s, but bygones are bygones and the country is now steadfastly bilingual. The life of the Swedish-speaking minority is in many respects better than that of their Finnish counterparts: Finn-Swedes live longer, suffer less

unemployment and divorce less than Finnish-speakers. They even have more children.

Nevertheless, the proportion of Finn-Swedes in Finnish society is continuously decreasing. During this century it's dropped by 50 %, from twelve to six per cent.

For centuries, perhaps for millenniums, Finns lived as large families, with many generations in one household. At the turn of this century it was still commonplace for a young bride to move in with her newly-wed, together with his sisters, parents and grandparents. Moving from the countryside to the town and adopting livelihoods other than farming have resulted in the virtual demise of the traditional large family. Nowadays, it's highly unusual for grandparents to live as part of their children's household. Young people

move away from their childhood homes to take up their studies. Finns spend their twilight years in old people's homes and community centres for the elderly.

At present, one in seven Finns is 65 or older. In 2010 the ratio will probably be one in five, and in 2020 one in four. Differences in the age structure between the more populated areas and remote communities are considerable: the further away from large towns one goes the more elderly people

there are. Many municipalities are having to face the harsh reality of adjusting to an increasing population and a diminishing workforce.

The rural depopulation of the 1960s contributed much to Finland's shortage of apartments. This problem is still the focus of endless committees.

Owning your own property has always been the norm in Finland and, as a rule, people tend to purchase their first apartment before they have completed their studies. The availability of rented apartments has long been wanting and rents often extortionately high. The market for rented accommodations has nonetheless picked up in recent years. This has led to more widespread availability and lower prices. The young in particular are interested in renting, since they have very little problem in finding more enjoyable ways of spending money.

Households plough a whopping quarter of their total expenditure into dwellings, and yet living space only works out at some thirty square metres per inhabitant. Practically a third of the population can be considered to be living in rather cramped conditions, meaning that there is more than one person per room in the same apartment. Over 50 % of Finns live in detached houses and approximately a third in apartments. Row houses are rapidly enjoying increased popularity.

Refrigerators, vacuum cleaners, colour televisions and phones are found in almost every home. Finns have also acquired a variety of other household appliances to ease the strain of everyday living: four out of five households have a washing-machine and freezer, and almost as many have microwave ovens. An electric

sewing machine and video recorder can be found in over half. And then, of course, there's the mobile phone. This meteoric mod-con has won special favour with Finns: one in five people walk around with one in his or her pocket.

Four out of ten Finns have their own car. New cars are expensive in Finland, hence their scarcity compared to other motorized countries. The average life-span of a  car is fourteen years. Most Finns could easily get to work without using their own cars since workplaces are usually less than three kilometres away from home.

Class differences between different social groups became less evident after the second world war. The differences that do exist can be more easily determined in terms of lifestyles as opposed to net incomes. As in the other Nordic countries, the Finnish welfare state, with its public health service, child-care service, unemployment benefits and pension systems has been so comprehensive that nobody has had to live in genuine poverty. There are, of course, considerable income disparities, but basic needs are well catered for, regardless of economic circumstance. The concept of poverty is nonetheless with us. People talk of the nouveau pauvre, who have lived beyond their means on all-too-easily-attainable loans, only to run into financial hardship or ruin.

 Class differences are probably at their the most evident in matters of death. People who work in physically taxing and badly-paid jobs die prematurely. On the other hand, the highly-educated tend to live longer. Unemployment and mortality, however, do not seem to have a causative relationship.

Education is highly respected in Finland. People are more interested in each others' level of education than they are in their monthly salary. The most esteemed professions are jurisdiction, medicine and teaching.

 And this, despite the fact that the level of income in many other professions can be considerably higher. Finns tend not to address each other as Mr. or Ms. very often, but titles and degrees are obligatory in correspondence.

The industrial growth of the 1960s also opened up large-scale job opportunities for women. The 90s has seen the majority of mothers with children under seven years of age working outside the home. This has resulted in considerable pressure being exerted on  communal daycare. The law stipulates that there must be a daycare place for anyone who needs it. A child under seven years old spends from eight to nine hours a day in a day nursery or a private family playgroup outside the home. When children reach the age of six there's pre-school, and at the age of seven they put on their backpacks and toddle off to school.

The average age for getting married is 27. Nearly 50,000 people hit the matrimonial trail every year. And almost a half of the marriages end up in divorce. Every seventh family is a single-parent family. It's very common for couples to live together before marrying. Cohabitation is considered a stable way of cementing a relationship. Unfortunately, statistics prove that it's even less durable than marriage. The

average family has less than two children. Only a few per cent of families have more than four children. This phenomenon is pan-European and can be explained, in part, by the growing ambitions of women in educational studies and working life. It's fairly common for a Finnish mother to be over 30 before she has her first child.

The most popular pastime is physical pursuits. Winter is mainly a time for cross-country or downhill skiing. Ice-skating is also popular with the young. Summer is a time for walking, jogging, biking, sailing and swimming. The country abounds in water, so nearly every Finn can swim. Reading is also very popular: on average, Finns loan 17 books per year from the library – an unofficial world record! Library books are available to all and there are regular library buses with over 20,000 scheduled stops.

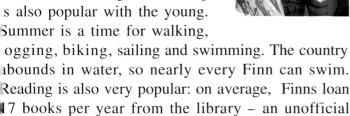

Nearly two-thirds of leisure time is spent at home and the most popular way of relaxing is by watching TV. Finns over ten years old spend around two and a half hours a day in front of the television.

It's almost a cliché to say that Finns are shy and reserved. The reality, however, is that Finns share exactly the same characteristics as any other people. There are, undoubtedly, regional differences: Eastern

Finns are noted for their liveliness and sociability whereas their Western counterparts are often considered slightly more reticent. And it has to be said that the Finnish psyche is somewhat melancholic; a result perhaps of long winters. In reality this melancholic tendency manifests itself in the depressingly high suicide rate.

When comparing themselves to other cultures Finns invariably bring up what they believe to be the originality of Finnish drinking patterns. The myth is that Finns drink rarely and then only in order to get drunk. When this is achieved they then behave loutishly, even violently. Nowadays, however, more and more citizens have a very restrained, 'European' relationship with alcohol.

In terms of church attendance Finns can certainly not be considered as being very religious. Nevertheless, some 90 per cent of the population do belong to the church, and four out of five consider themselves Christians. Baptism is very popular, as are church weddings and burials on church grounds.

Parliament House, completed in 1931, is symbolic of an independent Finland. It was designed by the architect, J.S. Sirén.

The National Museum in the background represents an older, national-romantic style and displays all the aspects of Finnish history.

Finland's independent status, granted under Russian reign, is symbolized by the Bank of Finland's massive facade. In the foreground: the statue of J.V. Snellman.

The Assembly House of the Estates (bottom) is situated across the street. This was where parliamentary sessions were held and decisions of national importance revealed.

The view from the South Harbour to Kruunuvuorenselkä (top) has remained unchanged for nearly a century. In the foreground: the restaurant islands of Valkosaari and Klippan; open to all. In the distance: the unique church tower of Suomenlinna (Sveaborg).

Kallio (in Helsinki) (bottom left), is the most densely-populated urban district in Finland. In the background: Kallio church, designed by Lars Sonck.

Merihaka, a cluster of living quarters and offices (bottom right) represents a 70s view of an urbane milieu.

Top left: Pikku-Huopalahti, set in a snug little cove opposite Munkkiniemi, represents one of the most recent solutions for city construction.

Bottom left: Mannerheimintie, one of the main routes in Helsinki, reveals all the aspects of business, democracy, culture and city life.

A tradition of making the most out of the sea lives on, both in the Kauppatori docks (top right) and on the Kaivopuisto shoreline (bottom right).

Helsinki's most intriguing sightseeing walk starts from Kauppatori, meanders along the shoreline at Kaivopuisto and ends up at Hietalahti marketplace.

Strolling around Töölönlahti is another nice walk. Starting from the east shore, the views from the summer terrace of a hundred-year-old villa reveal Helsinki's latest cultural enterprize; Finland's National Opera House (above).

A photograph of Eila Hiltunen's Sibelius monument in Taivallahti (bottom), is probably the most popular holiday snap taken by tourists in Finland.

Top: a view of Kauppatori marketplace at night, from Esplanade. Helsinki's endearing Esplanade is made up of a busy business street; Pohjoisesplanadi (North Esplanade); the slightly quieter Eteläesplanadi (South Esplanade), and the park area in between.
Bottom: Kappeli has undergone several phases during its hundred-year history. It's one of the capital's most popular restaurants, especially during the summer.

The King of Sweden and Finland, Gustavus Vasa,
founded Helsinki (Helsingfors) in 1550.
Initially, the town was located further to the north,
on the mouth of the River Vantaa.
Half a century later its centre was moved
to the Viro peninsula.
At the end of the 18th century it had 3,000
inhabitants and in 1812, when Alexander I
declared the town the capital of Finland, the figure
had risen to about 4,000.
After that, growth accelerated
considerably and by 1906 the number of
inhabitants had already reached 100,000.
Nowadays, Helsinki is Finland's only city
in the real sense of the word, but its night-life
is still relatively quiet.

Helsinki's
suburbs vary in
style and age.
Top left: Pikku-
Huopalahti from
the 1990s.
Top right:
Wooden Käpylä
from the 1920s.
Middle left:
Haukilahti, in
Espoo, is known
for its affluent
row houses,

whereas Tapiola
has developed
from a 1950s
garden suburb
(bottom)
to a densely
built-up district
(middle right).

A historical sight, the fortress islands of Suomenlinna (Sveaborg) lie just off Helsinki on the open sea. The fortifications were built at the end of the 1700s, under the direction of August Ehrensvärd. Originally, the fortress was intended to protect Sweden's eastern border, but it badly neglected its defence task during the Finland War and surrendered to the Russians on May 6th, 1808.

Nevertheless, it still stands as a unique site for museums and recreation areas, not to mention cultural events such as open-air summer theatre productions and Nordic art centre exhibitions.

Turku Cathedral has been under construction
for almost 800 years.
It has been endlessly elevated, extended;

its windows blocked in in the process; damaged
by fire and war and repaired time and time again.
The end result is monumental.

The building of Turku Castle began in 1280, when Sweden decided it needed a governmental castle for its representative in Finland.
It was frequently extended, changed and repaired after wars.
The most recent restoration work was carried out in 1961.
The architecture of the castle follows the lines of the Teutonic order and Vadstena.
Its list of inhabitants makes impressive reading: ranging from the Swedish Duke Charles to Gustavus Adolfus II and Pietari Brahe.
In the 17th century the castle lost its original status and was left to dilapidate.
The 19th century saw it used as a prison.

The restoration plan, started by the architect, Erik Bryggman, was meticulously adhered to. The aim was simply to restore its original atmosphere.

The area containing Turku was originally an archipelago, rising from the sea long ago. Nowadays, its islands stand as hills among its clay plains; its centre split in two by the River Aura. Even amidst all the traffic Paavo Nurmi demonstrates his faith in the Olympic ideal. Some Art Nouveau and finely-worked wooden houses still remain, though intensive building in the centre has paid its toll.

This mansion, donated by Ester and Mauno Vanhalinna to the University of Turku, houses a museum which perpetuates the primeval history and archaeological findings of South-West Finland. The Vanhalinna Museum in included in the European Council's Viking route sites.

25

Rauma is one of Finland's
oldest towns; its town charter
dating from the 1440s.
But even before then it was a busy
trading and religious centre,
hosting a Franciscan monastery.
The town hall, designed
by J. Sytten, was built in 1776.
The Church of the Holy Cross is
reminiscent of the monastery of
the 15th century.
Rauma's picturesque wooden
houses, located in its old-town
precinct, have been protected
by Unesco.

Naantali is one of the few towns in Finland founded during the Middle Ages. Its old town resembles an 18th century museum, both in regards to plan and buildings. Recent constructions in the town centre have been carried out thoughtfully and tastefully. Naantali also boasts the official summer residence of the Finnish president, Kultaranta.

The town of Salo was built in the remotest corner of Halikko Bay. Modern construction has done little to damage the wooden houses of previous generations.

A stone church, dating from 1831, and designed by C.L. Engel, looms elegantly above all the other buildings.

Hanko has always been a place for letting your hair down. It's an ideal place for tourists to hang loose in, too, since it hosts over 400 events during the summer months. If you're more interested in peace and quiet and bit of privacy then you'd be better off exploring the islets that follow Hanko's shoreline.

Finland's largest marina has over 400 mooring places. The yachts, together with the town's quaint old streets, are a veritable feast for the eye. The town is blessed with so much sea front that if every Finn were given a square metre of it nobody would have to settle further away than 30 metres from the water.

Timber barns – just one example of vanishing folk tradition. Nevertheless, they can still be found around Pietarsaari.

Was it the flatness of the views that made people long for far-off lands? The ship-building tradition in Pietarsaari started in the middle of the 17th century, about the same time as the town was founded. Europe's numerous shipyards were in dire need of tar and pitch in order to combat decay. And in order to transport the tar, ships were needed for charter. Hence the need for boatyards. Baltic Yacht, the largest on its field, still carries on the tradition.

Pietarsaari, with its 18th century craftsmen's quarters, 19th century rectangular street layout and early 20th century Jugendstil houses; interspaced with examples of more modern constructions dating back to the fifties; is

virtually a living museum.
Even the town's emblem was derived from architecture: the tobacco factory's clock.

Antti Chydenius, Kokkola's minister, started documenting his thoughts on economic Liberalism in 1765.
A busy port, together with Kemira and Outokumpu factories are modern-day legacies of Chydenius's writings. His idea had been to free the movement of production and goods from

the stringent controls of the state.
This, in turn, invigorated industry and trade.

Kokkola's town hall and many wooden buildings breath out a healthy respect for old values.

Alahärmä, situated in
the plains of East Bothnia
(in Western Finland)
was once notorious for
harbouring the bad men
of the parish; men whose main
claim to fame was through
their knives.
Ekola house is a prime example
of the kind of grandeur and
independence that has often
been associated with
East Bothnia.
It even has a sawmill to
provide itself with its own

construction materials.
Fur farming is a common
source of livelihood
in East Bothnia.
The picture shows foxes
at Ekola farm as well as
mink farms at Jepua,
a neighbouring parish.

East Bothnia's two-storey buildings have been standing proudly for a couple of hundred years. Top: Ruona houses in Kuortane.

Roads and railways lead to Seinäjoki from nearly every direction. The town was built around a steel factory, constructed at the end of the 18th century.

Nowadays, it's dominated by Alvar Aalto's architecture, the highest point being Lakeuden Risti church, with its 65-metre high tower.

Finland is a sporting nation, so it's not surprising that so many airdomes have spring up all over the place. Seinäjoki is no exception.

A land
covered in forest

Finland is often accurately referred to as the country of thousands of lakes. Lakes make up a tenth of the country and when recently counted (for the first time) the official total reached over 100,000. They do not, however, contain a lot of water, since their total volume has been estimated to be around 250 cubic kilometres. In other words, all of Finland's lakes would fit into Lake Ladoga or Onega. In some districts of southern Finland lakes cover half of the land area, in the north considerably less. Forests characterize the scenery even more than lakes since their share of the land is 70 per cent. Cultivated land stands at only ten per cent.

Throughout its history Finland has been between the East and West, culturally as well as politically. Behind this lies 700 years as part of the Kingdom of Sweden as well as a century under Russian rule. And the struggle for national identity did not end with Finland being granted independence in December 1917. Today's Finn, however, has no problems with his map reading. To the west there's a 600 kilometre border with Sweden, to the north a 700 kilometre one with Norway, and to the east the Russian border, stretching 1,300 kilometres.

Finland's location on the Baltic Sea has played a predominant role in its development. Small wonder, considering there's about 1,100 kilometres of coastline. In actual fact, it would be much more if every bay, nook and islet were included. The Gulf Stream, though not without influence, is far away, so the sea is often frozen for most of the winter. This, of course, is not enough to prevent Finns from getting about and fishing, even in the depths of winter.

The terrain in Finland mainly comprises lowland, with the average elevation above sea level standing at only a hundred metres. Eastern Finland enjoys slightly higher elevation. Only the treeless mountains of Lapland can qualify as genuine mountains, and they're mainly located in the Northwestern 'arm' of Finland. The highest point is to be found on Mount Halti on the Norwegian border, 1,328 metres above sea level. There are around 40 peaks which are over 1,000 metres. Although the land in Finland is very flat and even, local variations in elevation can still be significant.

Finnish soil, in relation to its area, is extremely uniform. The mineral aggregate, one of the oldest in the world, mainly consists of granite and gneiss, Archaean bedrock. Around 100,000 years ago the land was covered with a thick layer of ice. When it melted, some 11,000 years ago, it left behind unique traces. Giant ice masses gouged deep tracks in even the hardest rock, forcing along with it massive

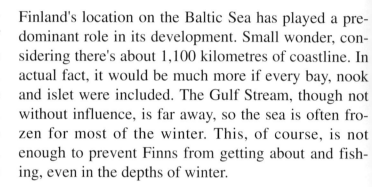

 erratic boulders. As the ice withdrew, ridges were born. These ridges are unique gravel formations, the most significant being Salpaus ridge, on the border of Finland's southeastern lake district. As the weight of ice over the ground diminished, so the push upwards began. Initially it was fast, but even today the land rises by nearly a centimetre a year on the coast of the Gulf of Bothnia. So, in a very real sense, Finland is the Daughter of the Baltic.

Apart from its firmness the Finnish lithosphere is also without comparison in terms of its thickness. The rock shield under us is invariably 35–40 kilometres thick. At the time of the ancient collision of the continental plateaus the thickness of the rock element totalled 65 kilometres in some areas of Eastern Finland. This is quite a figure since only the Himalayas can boast such a sturdy basis.

Only when the ice withdrew did the plants appear: at first bryophytes, lichens, grasses and twigs, shortly followed by the birch.  Since the earth in Finland is hard for the most part and the growing season short, the vegetation has remained relatively rugged. The tree stand in Finland largely belongs to the coniferous forest belt, with its characteristic pines and spruces. Only the birch can outmatch the tenacious conifers. It's the pioneer of Finnish trees and the dwarf birch variety is the only tree that grows in Lapland's mountain areas. In the south, the predominant tree is the spruce.

Further north, it's the pine. Throughout Finland the vividness of the birch brings variety to the otherwise dark hues of the coniferous forests. In the swamps and mountains of the country's northernmost parts it unsophisticatedly but grittily symbolizes Finnish persistence.

Considering how much of the country is situated inside the Arctic Circle there's very little arctic tundra to be found. The northern climate; long, cold and dark winters together with warm, light summers leaves its mark on trees and other vegetation: trees grow relatively slowly and branches remain short.

 In the winter the frail branches break under the weight of snow and even sturdier ones buckle under their strain.

In the last century, the burning-over of woodland for cultivation, tar burning, coal production, shipbuilding, timber exporting and the development of the forest industry thinned out the woods to such an extent that some were already being kissed goodbye. All the way up until the 1970s forest resources remained very stable, neither increasing nor decreasing. The timber reserve was 1,500–1,600 million cubic metres. Over the last two decades or so the increasingly efficient forest improvement and silviculture measures have resurrected Finnish timber reserves. The 2,000 million cubic metre limit will, in all probability, be exceeded before the year 2000.

When you sit on a plane on the way from Helsinki to Rovaniemi, all you see is forests and swamps.

There are so many swamps that you could say that they're second only to forests. Nowadays, the beauty of untouched swampland - marshes, fens and bogs - can be appreciated in any of Finland's 30 national parks. For centuries, they were despised rather than admired: there was too much swamp, not enough field. Fires burning over a buried treasure pit, fairies prancing around and frost rising, all these were images relating

to swamps. Many of the swamps were drained and peat gathered from them. Hence, their significance in terms of the country's prosperity: nowadays, over 100,000 tonnes of peat is exported to around 30 countries.

In the coniferous forest the shadow of the trees does not allow much undervegetation. It's in the lighter groves, meadows, headlands and alongside rivers that one meets the full spectrum of flowers and bushes. The abundance of wild berries is magnificent. Every Finn has been berry-picking at least once, gathering into buckets bilberries, arctic whortleberries, wild strawberries and raspberries. More fortunate individuals will have found the cloudberry, the cranberry and even the arctic bramble. Almost considered an art form, mushroom-picking at its best can demand detailed knowledge of tens of different varieties of mushroom. The most delicious and edible mushrooms, the false morel and chanterelle, are familiar to everyone.

The animals that feature in ancient Finnish fables are still very much with us. Over 100,000 elk have been

counted in Finnish forests. The elk, with its stately antlers, is good to keep in mind, considering the number of traffic signs that warn us of them. Nature lovers could just as easily come across a fox, hare, lynx, wolf or bear, or even a wolverine in the north. Finns are especially proud of their white-tailed eagle and the ringed seal – both protected species.

If Finns were to vote on the most unpopular creature the undisputed winner would be the mosquito. These bloodthirsty insects can spoil even the most beautiful summer's day. They're often at their most prolific during midsummer. They can then disappear for weeks, only to return as the weather begins to cool down. The Lapps, who have had to live with these tiny nuisances for centuries, have long since become immune to their bite.

In Lapland hundreds of families belonging to the indigenous population, the Lapps, gain their livelihood from reindeer management. Reindeer management, which nowadays centres on meat production, already

began in the late Middle Ages. Finns, too, have managed reindeer for some 200 years. Today, there are around 200,000 reindeer in Finland. Forest animals are exploited in other ways in Finland. The west coast in particular is home to several large fur farms, where minks and foxes are raised, destined for the

international fur trade. The annual fur auction in Vantaa is the world's biggest, and purchasers come from as far afield as the Far East.

Finnish waters have largely remained clean enough to swim in. The Finnish fish population is extremely varied and abundant in many places. The most common fish are burbot, trout, pike, whitefish and perch, but many a fisherman travels all the way to Lapland's famous salmon fishing grounds. And the catch is invariably well worth the effort.

Pollution is also a reality in Finland, though compared with many industrial regions in Central Europe the country can appear almost virginally clean. As in most other European countries, people's awareness of the environment has increased in recent years. Concern about the state of the environment is not purely a trendy subject for conversation. On the contrary;

inland waters, groundwater, soil and air have been actively protected. All the coastal states on the Baltic Sea have cooperated in an effort to save the sea.

Society protects the environment in various ways. The state levies all kinds of taxes for actions which stress the environment, covering everything from water-pollution control charges and oilwaste duties, to a tax on non-returnable bottles and, at great annoyance to motorists, a car tax. In a genuine effort to enforce protection regulations, hundreds of plant and animal species have been allocated a specific monetary value. Over a tenth of the Finnish forests are protected by law. Waste legislation has been tightened up and more and more people have had to get used to sorting out their household waste. A great deal has also been done as regards the protection of parks in densely built-up areas.

The clear majority of Finns accept the protection of the environment by statutory law. Theoretically, they could even accept a situation which would inhibit freedom of choice. Even more people want to see controls on pollution emissions being tightened up and made more extensive. When Finns go shopping their choice is often effected by how environmentally-friendly the products are. Environmental aspects have therefore penetrated the infrastructure of business life.

Saarijärvi was originally made famous for Finns
by J.L. Runeberg.

The cupola in the Empire church, designed by
C.L. Engel, is the largest in Finland.

41

Tampere is the largest inland city
in the Nordic Countries.
It's situated on a neck of land
between Lake Näsi and Lake Pyhä.
This old workers' town, located
by the Tammer rapids, has often
given birth to personalities of
cultural significance.
Tampere is particularly famous
for its many authors; ranging from
Lauri Viita to Väinö Linna.

The city took shape in the 17th
century around three mansions
and their surrounding crofts.
In 1779, Gustavus III granted
Tampere a town charter.
Since then, it has steadily
developed to such an extent that
it has regularly competed with
Turku for the distinction
of being
Finland's
second
largest city.

Tampere's emergence as one of Finland's most important industrial centres began at the end of the 1820s, when a Scotsman, James Finlayson, founded a cotton mill on the shore of Tammer rapids.
The city centre was completed about 100 years ago, in neoclassical, NeoRenaissance and national romantic styles.

Even the Finnish Government has made an effort to protect Tampere's historical centre, under threat from the efficiency of modern-day construction. The nostalgia of the city's heyday is still very much in evidence in its cityscape.
Nowadays, demands for growth have been absorbed by the suburbs.

As elsewhere, churches have always tried to reach for the sky, irrespective of landscape.

Typical examples are Kangasala's medieval stone church and Tampere's Kalevankangas modern functionalistic church.

Although recorded history in Finland is short compared with the rest of Europe, there are churches dating back to the Middle Ages – and that includes those in Northern Finland.

The stone walls in Pälkäne's medieval church ruins have braved the test of time. Abundant tile decoration reveal the original wealth of the area.

The original builders of Häme castle would never have believed that a human being could one day fly above the castle, as free as a bird. In those days only a bird could get into the castle without being stopped since it was surrounded by water. Over centuries, constant elevation of the land has left water on only one shore, in the Linnasalmi (channel) of Vanajavesi.

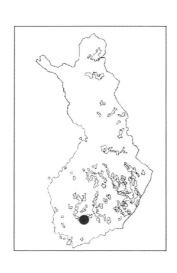

After doing the laundry all day or enjoying some light exercise there's no better place to cool down in than the ship restaurant.

The long recession in the building trade has fortunately not meant the demise of small sawmills. Export routes beyond Finland have remained open, keeping alive mills such as Ridasjärvi in Hyvinkää. Ritaspuu's busy sawmill floats down the logs from the barking plant and saws them into square timber, thick board, ordinary board and strips of wood.

Raw board is dried in the outer stacks and its humidity measured. The ends of the stacks resemble abstract paintings.

Summer in Finland is
a celebration of enjoyment.
To most Finns, Suonenjoki is
synonymous with strawberries.
Left: Raikanpelto farm in
Suonenjoki.

Linseed oil is a versatile substance:
a rot-resistant agent, paint binder,
anti-rust agent as well as a food
product – as demonstrated by
Pella-Tuote's entrepreneur.

Finland's EU membership means
that its now possible to make wine
from apples and berries for com-
mercial purposes.
Below: Anola vineyard
in Pieksämäki.

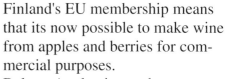

The shopmobile is always a much-
welcomed visitor, particularly in
remote areas.

These well-known storehouses are located by the banks of the River Porvoo and beside the oldest road in Finland. The road from Turku to Vyborg (in Russia) passed through the steepest street in Finland. Situated in Siltamäki in Porvoo, this stretch of road still leads towards the cathedral, built in the 14th century. This old timber town is looked after with tender loving care.

A view of the Porvoo's old town from Linnanmäki.

During the Crimean war Britain's
Royal Navy burnt down Finland's
coastal towns as fast as it could.
Loviisa, too, was burnt to the
ground in 1855.
The provincial architect,
G.Th. Chiewitz, designed the
NeoGothic town hall and church,
which was completed ten years
after the fire.
Idyllic wooden villas, situated in
the lower part of the town, are
more recent.

When Finland, under Sweden, ceded Hamina's border fortification to Russia under the terms of the Treaty of Turku, a new customs town was needed to control trade in the south-eastern part of the country. A site was chosen in an area which could be fortified.

This windmill, set beside a nuclear power plant reminds us that we have gone full circle: new energy sources are becoming scarce, while wind energy remains a durable alternative.

The construction of the Rosen and Ungen fortifications got underway in 1743. And the town was named after Queen Loviisa.

The island area between
the branches of River Kymi's
Huumanhaara and Langinkoski
had provided an important base
for eastern trade as long ago
as Viking times. The rise of the
sawmill industry, beginning in
the 1870s, led to the foundation of
the town of Kotka in 1878.
Kotka has a splendid natural
harbour and has consequently
become one of Finland's most
important ports of entry.
The port has also lured large-scale
industry to the town. Directly
above: Enso-Gutzeit's factory.

Modern-day Vikings on their way to picturesque
Haapasaari. Many more idyllic settings can be found
around the harbour park area.

Hamina is in fact the EU's easternmost port: there's a free warehouse there as well as a liquid port, which is the centre for the transit traffic of liquids.

Hamina also competes for first place as a timber shipping port. Hot lines and tight ropes are essential before ships depart with their raw-wood freight.

Kouvola railway station
was built in 1875
on the uninhabited
Salpaus ridge
as part of the
Riihimäki–St.Petersburg
railway section.
Building originally
concentrated around
the station and the area
underwent rapid growth
just as soon as Kouvola
became the crossroads
of four railways.

Such development
virtually steamrolled
its hundred years of
building history.

Finlandia

As early as the stone age Finns were a creative people and appreciative of beauty. The most famous indication of this is the Huittinen moose head, a sleek weapon from the preceramic period, over 1,000 years B.C. After the Stone Age, art was born out of the needs of ordinary people to mold their environment, furniture, textiles and tools so that things not only felt good but looked good. Many specimens of the work of these long-gone artists are on display in museums.

The Finns' ability to design beautiful everyday items has won them international recognition. Iittala glass and Fiskars scissors are esteemed throughout the world. Marimekko's fashions have been sold in the fanciest of locations.

The oldest remaining representatives of architecture are medieval castles and stone churches, together with their murals. Only a handful of centuries-old wooden buildings remain. Most of them have been destroyed by fire. Wooden houses have had to make way for more efficient buildings, especially in the towns. Helsinki was the capital of the Grand Duchy, and in due course received a grand Empire look to it during the 19th century. The forerunners of Finnish architecture in this century have been Eliel Saarinen and Alvar Aalto, both internationally acclaimed architects. The most recent outstanding work is Mäntyniemi, the official residence of the President. It was designed by Reima and Raili Pietilä.

The golden era of Finnish painting took place at the turn of the century. That was the time of such national romantics as Albert Edelfelt and Akseli Gallen-Kallela as well as Finland's most famous female painter, Helene Schjerfbeck. All of them had enormous influence on establishing the Finnish identity. Today's influential artists include the respected and productive cubist, Sam Vanni, and the neorealist, Kimmo Kaivanto.

Wäinö Aaltonen was the first sculptor since the ancient Egyptians to employ granite in his work. Two sculptors, both of them women, have achieved international acclaim - Eila Hiltunen with her welded steel creations and Laila Pullinen, who excels in bronze and copper.

The Finnish national epic, the Kalevala, was compiled by Elias Lönnrot and published in 1835. It has been translated into nearly 40 languages. The 'Seven Brothers' by Aleksis Kivi underwent a lot of criticism when it came out, but has been adored by all later generations. Finland's most internationally-acclaimed authors in the 20th century are F.E. Sillanpää, who received the Nobel price in 1939, Mika Waltari, who wrote 'Sinuhe the Egyptian', Väinö Linna, who expertly dealt with difficult topics in the recent history of the country, as well as the modern authors, Paavo Haavikko and Veijo Meri. Tove Jansson, the creator of the Moomin characters, is a favourite with millions of children and adults all over the world.

The legend of Finnish music is, of course, the master composer Jean Sibelius. The most famous expert Finnish musicians on the international circuit have been the opera singers, Martti Talvela, Matti Salminen, Jorma Hynninen and Karita Mattila, the pianist, Ralf Gothóni, the cellist, Arto Noras and the conductors, Paavo Berglund, Jorma Panula, Leif Segerstam, Okko Kamu and Esa-Pekka Salonen.

Our highly-original Finnish pop-music has not, as yet, enjoyed many international breakthroughs. One notable exception are the Leningrad Cowboys, who have received a global cult-following in the 1990s.

The central and western parts of Southern Finland are home to Finland's traditional festive drink, 'Sahti'. This home-brewed beer invariably starts its preparation in the sauna or in the boiling house, where there's an abundance of hot water close at hand.
Brewing beer takes time; the mist is already over the lake before fermentation is over.

People often say that they feel
as good as new after a sauna.
This reveals the ritualistic
properties of the sauna: in addition
to the body the soul also seems
to undergo cleansing.
And even if you are able
to wash your own back,
it feels twice as nice to have
someone else to do it for you.
So, that's another ritual,
not forgetting of course,
the ceremonial dive, jump
or dip into fresh water.

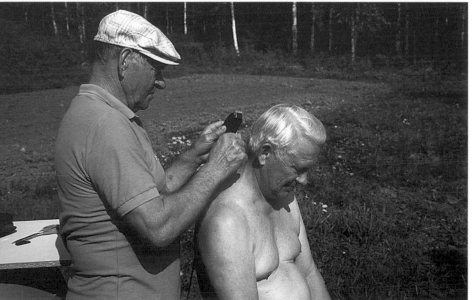

Anyone for a haircut? The tools of
the trade are conveniently hung
over the moped's handle bars.

Lahti was Finland's youngest and liveliest city
for more than a couple of decades.
In recent years dozens of new vibrant towns
have sprung up inside a single generation.
The closer you get to Lahti the more aware
you are of how important sports are there.
The success of Finnish ski jumpers is
a direct result of summertime practice.
And when ever there's a competition,
the town is as pulsating as an ant hill.

Sometimes Finland's friendly face has to undergo major surgery, so that cars can get people from place to place.

This section of road, which includes Heinola Star, Finland's longest bridge, is one of the country's busiest at weekends.

The old bridges have been left intact for the exclusive use of townsfolk.

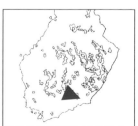

Heinola's lively marketplace is a genuine meeting place where all kinds of products change hands.

Age-old traditions of acting, performing music and drinking beer are celebrated on the

restaurant terraces as well as in the marketplace.

In medieval times market days were related to church festivals. Nevertheless, they were important trade events way up until the 20th century. The tradition is still upheld by Heinola's rural community. A children's market stall is a guarantee that the tradition will go on.

9,000 years ago the Yoldia Sea was billowing where Päijänne now stands.

Nowadays this old sea bed runs rich in crops in Toivakka's Viisarinmäki and turnip rape in Sysmä's Kalkkinen.

The last ice age ground away at this part of Sysmä for a hundred thousand years, yet it still left 221 metres worth of high land here in Kammiovuori, Eastern Häme's highest point. The views from the mountain are typical of the Finnish landscape.
A rolling stone gathers no moss.

The horse was long considered a sign of wealth in Finland. Its most important task was to help people with their work in the fields and woods.

The mechanization of agriculture and forestry meant that the very existence of the tough Finnish horse was under threat.

But the increased popularity of trotting, combined with rising living standards, meant that

Finnish horses were also bred for trotting purposes – even if it is the thoroughbreds that rule the day at the trotting-tracks. Kemppi's stallions in Asikkala.

A Finnish war-time song goes: "There's no hay for the horses, they'll have to eat the stable walls". Such scarcity is compensated for by efficient haymaking, where all are welcome to perform a sweaty but rewarding task. Hay dried on hay poles is sold to horse farms since horses don't take kindly to baled hay.

Hay fragments are cleared away in Sysmä's Kalkkinen with the help of some genuine home-brew. Home-brewed beer gives you energy in the heat of the summer's day.

Finland's short summer cannot compete
with those of southern Europe, with its two harvests.
Finland's forte is its natural purity.

Purity, which can be enjoyed in a variety of ways,
both in terms of agricultural products
and beautiful scenery.

Many a wily student has graduated from Evo Forestry Training School. It has a long tradition in taking care

of the park's 7,000 or more hectares. Forests give shelter to grazing cattle in the rain.

The largest forest and lake area designated for camping in the more densely-populated area of Finland can be found in Evo. Lure fishing is possible on several lakes, fishing licenses are readily available and boats are easily rented. Sleeping in a lumberjacks' cabin guarantees a genuine experience.

It has been said that the salt contained in human blood is primeval, a remnant of when our progenitors still lived in the sea.

Perhaps that's why Finns always need to be near water, close to Neptune's domain. Views from lake Päijänne.

Mikkeli, surrounded by a multitude
of lakes, was founded in 1838.
Its centre has undergone heavy
development over recent decades.
Fortunately, the town also has older
buildings, some of which date
back to the Middle Ages.

Wood or  high-tech

Industrialization started early but slowly in Finland. Even in the beginning of the 1950s a significant part of the population lived off farming and the forest. The development over the following decades was incredibly fast from a European perspective – only matched in velocity by the Far East. By the 1970s Finland had become a developed, post-industrial society with a steady annual growth of five per cent for a period of 25 years. Statistically speaking, at the end of the 1980s Finland was one of the five wealthiest countries in the entire world.

This meteoric change had its price. The countryside became deserted and lifestyles changed dramatically. Despite the safety nets set up by society many have experienced this new way of life, with no real contact  with those closest to them, a very distressing one. At the beginning of the 1990s, as the unemployment figures rose to nearly a half a million and there was no light on the horizon the uncertainty of personal income became a national issue. The simple fact is that the availability of jobs will never increase to the levels of yesteryear. And this, simultaneously combined with increasing economic expectations, represents a Pan-European phenomenon. It will lead to severe structural solutions in working life, even here in Finland.

The Finnish economy has been built on the principles of private ownership and free enterprise. Its vulnerability was long protected by limiting the impact of foreign trade conditions. Nowadays, however, it's market forces that dictate direction.

 Since internal Finnish markets are small, foreign trade has a crucial role in the creation of welfare. For many years foreign demand was mainly aimed at products relating to the wood processing industry. Since the middle of the 1940s, trade with Russia, which at its peak accounted for nearly a third of all exports, was fundamental in the creation of Finland's strong steel industry. Later on, new production areas such as our textile and clothing industry, chemical industry and electronics became established.

Nearly a third of the working population obtain their livelihood from industry and construction, nearly two-thirds from the service industry. Jobs in the agriculture and forest industries have decreased to less than a tenth. And as Finland adjusts to the European Union they will continue to decrease, as will the number of farms.

In agriculture, specialization and increasing farm size would seem to be the road to success. Nevertheless, even with imagination and a passion for enterprise, the youngest generation of many an old farming family will be forced to change their occupation.

Two-thirds of the population believes that Finland's social obedience will deteriorate and civil disturbance will result unless there's a curb in massive unemploy-  ment. However, nothing seems to stand in the way of Finland's traditional export areas; forest and steel. They still seem destined to continue growing. But it does look as if ever-increasing responsibility for employment will fall upon the mighty high-tech companies. Their flagship is, of course, Nokia, a company which has already conquered half the world with its mobile phones.

In this global village of ours, where everyone plays a part in competition in all areas of the economy, Finland not only has to be able to implement its traditional strengths, but also has to find the courage to invest in research and development in brand-new areas. It's unlikely ever to compete with prices – Finland must convince its clients in terms of its capability.

Jyväskylä, by Lake Jyväs, is situated in an area rich in cultural sights and peaceful countryside. Jyväskylä, situated in the centre of Finland´s lake district, has excellent bus connections to all parts of the country. Jyväskylä University´s Ylistönmäki complex is one of Finland´s newest university buildings.

Industry and waterways are characteristic of the town of Varkaus, in Central Savo. The town has developed around the Varkaus rapids, which as early as the Middle Ages acted as a trading centre. By the beginning of the 19th century industry, specifically ironworks and sawmills, nestled here. Enso-Gutzeit's factory (top).

77

The views in and around Leppävirta invariably feature its Empire-style stone church (left, far distance). It was designed by C.L. Engel and completed in 1846.

The area is a crossroads of waterways, roads and Saimaa's deep channel,

making it an ideal location for tourist in need of relaxation.

Lignell & Piispanen's bottled products from Kuopio.

Puijo tower revolves
on its own axis.
Locals feel that life revolves
around Kuopio marketplace.
Lake Kallavesi looms
on the horizon.
From there you can embark
on your own boat trip all the way
to the Gulf of Finland.

'Kalakukko' – the Finnish fish
pasty – is an ingenious packaging
concept: you simply eat the
wrapping together with the meal.

Kalakukko.

Iisalmi is the heart of Savo dialect and culture (top).

The world's smallest restaurant, Korkki (Finnish for cork) can be found in the town's port.
It only has room for one customer, but if the weather's nice then there's plenty of room for one more on the terrace.

The Nordic countries' one and only brewery museum can be found in the old customs house, next to the restaurant. Donated by the local Olvi brewery, the museum's restaurant boasts a vast can collection, a small fraction of which can be seen here.

Kajaani, located by the
River Kajaani in the cove
of Lake Oulu, is
the business, industrial
and cultural centre
of the Kainuu area.
Kainuu has always been
extremely capable in
the utilization of its vast
woodlands.
Tar was taken by row boat
to Oulu from the beginning
of the 19th
century onwards.

Its woodlands produce
an abundance of berries;
an annually renewable
resource.

Let Finns
be Finns

Many ideas have been put forward as to who the Finns are originally. For over a hundred years they were taught, in the truly romantic and nationalistic spirit of the 19th century, that the original home of their Finnish ancestors lay in the bend of the Volga. The roots of the Finnish language would seem to be essentially eastern, Uralian perhaps. But according to current beliefs the origins of the Finn vary from the Volga region to central Europe and even the British Isles. As long ago as 4,000 B.C. Proto-Finno-Ugric was not only spoken in Finland but also in Northern Germany, all of Scandinavia, the Baltic Countries as well as in the Volga and Ural regions. The continental glacier withdrew towards the north, somehow enticing the Finns along with it. It's highly improbable that any dramatic migration of peoples took place. More likely, it was an arduous and gradual migration, covering tens of generations.

Some three-quarters of the Finnish genotype is Baltic-Germanic, i.e. Indo-European, only a quarter is Eastern. Even more surprising, perhaps, is that the people closest to the Finns genotypically are the Belgians. But there again, their Scandinavian neighbours or the Germans are not exactly unrelated. The Lapps, however, are considerably more different genetically, despite the relatively close proximity of the Finnish and Lapp languages.

The earliest prehistoric findings on the Finnish

peninsula are post ice age, dating back some 10,000 years ago. Finns lived here, fishing and hunting for thousands of years, continuously adapting their habitat to the migratory patterns of their quarry. Farming colonization became permanent and continuous in the western part of the Finnish peninsula during the Iron Age, i.e. somewhere around 50–400 A.C. Numerous place names, Germanic in origin, such as Masku, Piikkiö, Perniö and Rymättylä, are vested remnants of that period. Trade connections slowly took shape, initially around the Baltic Sea, then later on a wider scale. Trade consisted furs. Payment in kind took the form of fabrics and precious metals. Language and cultural influences also underwent change. During the time of the Vikings trade picked up along the eastern route of the Varangians. Some Finns joined these civilized savages, mostly as a wife or a rower, but hardly of their own accord.

Christianity spread furtively throughout the country, slowly and bloodlessly. There was no cause to enforce the belief by the sword. Judging from writings of the times, Christian influence, presumably in the form of legends and habits, had been filtered through to regions west of the Gulf of Bothnia since the 6th century. In Viking times the Christian influence subsided for a while and the belief became popularized As a result, the crusades of 1155, 1238 and 1292 witnessed the building of many a castle or outpost in

various parts of the country. With the help of the papacy and Swedish weaponry the Finnish Christians managed to defend themselves against the pagans and the orthodox Novgorodians. A pact between Catholic Finns and Swedes was sealed in the Treaty of Pähkinäsaari in 1323, under which Finland's central areas were ceremoniously decreed as being under the

jurisdiction of the Church of Rome, pertaining to the west and part of the Swedish Empire. Karelia was left as a Novgorod bastion; an eastern outpost.

Finland, Sweden's eastern province, was ruled by Finns, with the joint blessing of the King of Sweden and the Archbishop of Upsala. Finns were also allowed a say in their choice of king, since as early as 1362 they were allowed to take part in the regal elections on the Mora Stone. The most powerful figures were the nobility and the clergy, headed by the bishop of Turku who was also Master of Kuusisto castle.

In the 16th century, Gustavus Vasa, the King of Sweden, made special efforts to ensure that his empire was united and strong. An affluent and degenerate church and Finnish aristocracy, which repeatedly schemed its own political infiltration was a far cry from the royal plan. The Reformation took effect within the empire; the church lost its riches and the Finnish moguls lost their stronghold. Henceforth, the official proclamation followed the interest of the state itself. Hundreds of bailiffs, officials, priests and soldiers journeyed to Finland, to enforce it. Even the king's son, John, held his grand renaissance court in Turku castle.

In consolation for the loss of special status, the Finns

were allowed to have their own written language. Priests had been writing down religious texts in Finnish for some time. But it was left to Mikael

Agricola, student of Wittenberg (the town of Luther) and one of Finland's most significant travellers, to institutionalize Finnish as a written language. This he accomplished with the printing of his Prayer Book in 1544.

Even before Agricola, since the 14th century, Finns had found their way to European universities, including Paris and Prague. The academic accomplish-

ments of Finnish students were by no means insignificant and some even got as far as being vice-chancellors of the Sorbonne. The Reformation, however, closed the gates to the Quartier Latin and the spring of Prague. Consequentially, Germany became the new centre of academia. In actual fact, and despite the influence of Gustavus Vasa, the trend had already been heading in this direction for a century.

The Thirty Years´ War also offered Finns an opportunity to travel abroad. Between 1618 and 1648 a total of 48,000 Finnish men fought in Poland and the Baltic countries on Sweden´s behalf. The most legendary were the cavalry. Many died, some returned. Their souvenirs included tobacco and fresh ideas. The bellicose epoch under Swedish rule wore down the country in many ways. In return, they offered spiritual reward and, to a fortunate few, material gain.

In the great Pohja War, between 1700 and 1721, the young King Charles XII of Sweden took his mighty army to foreign lands, forfeiting his powerful empire in the process and finally his life in Norway. The king's preoccupation with the west provided Peter the Great with easy access to establish a new capital by the mouth of the river Neva, on Sweden's Finnish soil. He also invaded Finland itself and captured the city of Vyborg together with the entire southeast of the country. This loss was to prove to be a bitter bone of contention for future Swedish kings, but they found no solace in revenge. In 1809, during the Napoleonic Wars, the whole of Finland fell to Russia. As an autonomous grand duchy, its position was strong.

The people's loyalty smoothly switched from the King of Sweden to the new Czar. This was achieved by summoning the estates and promising continued recognition of the Lutheran faith as well as the existing judicial system and social order. The latter two secured, the Czar then set about securing the loyalty of Finland's elite through a policy of flattery; featuring decorations of honour, awards and official letters raising their status to that of a nobility as well as wage increases.

For nearly a century the Finns were able to live, build on their land and generally go about their own business in an unprecedented period of peace. The Czar's formal representative was a Russian governor-general. He presided in Turku, the capital of his borderland.

*Runeberg´s statue
in Esplanadi Park.*

However, from 1812 onwards he took office in Helsinki. In practice, the power was held by the senate, consisting entirely of Finns. If someone had something to say to the Czar, the Ministerial Secretary of State acted as a representative. Finland was allowed to define its own customs control at its borders and yet, at the same time, export its products to Russia almost duty-free. And this, combined with the practically inexhaustible demands of St. Petersburg alone provided the basis for economic strengthening and the birth of industry.

Finland started to turn into something far different from what Alexander I had originally had in mind when he had granted it autonomy. Increased prosperity, partly at the expense of its mother country, brought with it greater ambitions for self-determination. Lönnrot compiled the Kalevala as the Finnish national epic. Runeberg and Topelius created the concept of the fatherland. Snellman promoted the Finnish language to share equal status with Swedish and saw his dream of the country having its own currency turn into reality. The spiritual distances between Finland and Russia, and Finland and Sweden were also increasing.

This grand duchy, situated beside the city of the Czar, with its ever-increasing prosperity and pride, irritated the panslavists simply by being there. The panslavists had acquired a great deal of power in Russia at the end of the 19th century. What was this province, where neither Russian money nor stamps were accepted, and where no Russian citizen could be appointed to office? Wasn't the point of having a borderland one of guaranteeing the security of the empire's safety, not of challenging it? From a Russian point of view

these questions were good and justifiable. Cancellation of those benefits originally granted to Finland got underway. These were then replaced by unification; Russification. At first it took the form of the occasional administrative action but, following the imperial manifesto of February, 1899, it became meticulous and specific in design. In a futile attempt to stop the policy of oppression, a young patriot called Eugen Schauman shot dead the governor-general, Nikolai Bobrikov, and then himself. But the period of oppression certainly did not end there. The general strike of 1905 also failed to succeed; a mere hiccup in Russian eyes. Then came the First World War, the Russian Revolution and, amidst all this turmoil, somewhat unexpectedly, independence – in December 1917.

By the summer of that year, the revolution in Russia

and the famine were causing chaos in the forms of demonstrations, strikes, looting, and fighting. Ramifications were also felt in Finland. The country was rapidly becoming divided, into the whites and the reds. The most radical wanted Finland to have its own revolution. Finland's independence did nothing to remove such conflict, in fact it only aggravated the situation. In 1918 Finland had its War of Independence, also referred to as the War of Liberation or the Finnish Civil War. In May, after a bloody and vicious struggle, the victorious whites marched to Helsinki, led by their supreme commander, General Mannerheim. Thousands of reds were put into prisoner camps or disposed of by execution squads. The country was supposed to become a kingdom, but after the fall of Germany in the First World War, the prince who had been invited to be the first King of Finland thought better of it and decided to stay put in Hessen. Hence, Finland became a republic, where the presidency had enormous powers.

During its first decade of independence Finland was probably at its most independent. Russia had been considerably weakened by the war and internal struggles, and Germany had been humiliated in Versailles, so Finland had to get by all on its own. The non-socialist political tolerance of the country did not

exactly extend to its communists, the extraparliamentary successors of the reds of 1918. But the social democrats were not excluded; they were even let into the government and allowed to hold office, even up to the level of prime minister. To the right lay extremists who dreamed of a Great Finland. They were left alone to hallucinate until 500 of the most extreme ones started a mutiny. Their effort failed but opened many people's eyes. And so this young democracy stumbled but did not fall.

Finland began to feel isolated as soon as the first sign of a major new war raised its ugly head. It decided to

turn to the Nordic countries, but they showed no enthusiasm to reciprocate. So, on November 30th, 1939 and without a declaration of war, Russian bombers showered death onto the centre of Helsinki. This was simply an indication of Stalin's ruthless

policy of spheres of interest. This tiny country had to defend itself against an overwhelming enemy. Its only ally was winter. Finland went to war intact and totally united. It fought for 105 days, humiliated the Red Army, conceded to the punishing terms of peace, but kept its independence. Things had not quite gone as Moscow had planned. This had been Finland's Winter War.

In 1941 a new war started, this time it was fought all over the world. Now it was Finland's turn to attack. It

regained the regions it had lost and then pressed on. In the summer of 1944 it withdrew, at times fighting rear-guard action, at others simply running. By the autumn the Finnish defence had become so much stronger that the Red Army stopped, it had run out of time. A peace was arrived at, which offered even worse conditions than the previous agreement. Nevertheless, it was tolerable.

The country was led by new faces; unsoiled, in the eyes of Moscow. There were not a great many alternatives. Necessity was made a virtue and people began learning how to live with their old enemy as an eastern neighbour. In politics this meant a policy of non-provocation. Finland's economy made the most of its trading opportunities with Eastern Europe. During the split reality of the cold war Finland stuck firmly to its neutrality. Secretly, it felt it belonged to the west but what was the point in telling anyone.

In 1956 the Soviet Union returned the Porkkala base to Finland, which it had leased on the grounds of the peace treaty. This was meant as a gesture of goodwill and confidence in Finland's new foreign policy. The

anxiety that had been felt among state leaders and citizens alike disappeared overnight. After all, a Russian base within firing range of the president's palace had hardly had a calming effect on people's nerves.

That same year saw Urho Kekkonen being elected as president of the republic. This event repeated itself in 1962, in 1968, in 1974 (under emergency law) and even in 1978. This controversial figure regally directed Finland's foreign and internal policy when

and how he pleased. In 1975 he brought 35 state leaders to Helsinki to agree on safety and cooperation of Europe. This man, known as "Urkki" to his people, slowly made himself irreplaceable. When this wily and weary soul resigned in the autumn of 1981 the unre-

placeable had to be replaced. Koivisto's era started.

The world changed so much in the 1980s that even the impossible became possible. Finland had always managed the art of the possible. When the moment proved provident the country broke off its relationship with the east, established through war and peace. Now it was on its own again, as in the early years of its independence. It had freedom of choice. Finland decisively chose its own direction; westward. It was not in need of a military pact, more one of a political and economic nature. The obvious choice was the European Union.

As nations, Sweden and Denmark outdate Finland by over a thousand years. Nevertheless, the country still figures in the third oldest independent states, meaning there are over 130 states younger than Finland. In 1919, two years after independence, the country got its constitution. It's still in force, and for the most part, unchanged.

The constitution and its traditionally rigid adherence are indicative of the solid status of western democracy and parliamentarism. The relationship between the highest branches of government and the basic rights of the individual are practically carved in stone.

In Finland all power is vested with the people, represented by a unicameral parliament. Every four years the people choose their 200 representatives by direct vote. In 1995, 22 parties nominated their own candidates. Ten of these were successful in getting their representatives elected.

The parliamentary representatives are not, of course, representative of a cross section of the Finnish population. They have a higher income, more property and a superior education, as well as heavier loans. Their

income was three and a half times greater than and their loans twice as much as the average citizen's. 140 of the 200 held a university degree. There were not that many unemployed, pensioners or students to be found among them.

Finland was the first country in Europe to grant women the right to vote and the opportunity of becoming a candidate in political

elections. Women first voted in the parliamentary elections of 1906. Since then their participation in political decision-making has steadily increased. So has their share of parliamentary seats.

The President of the Republic is the chief executive and has considerable powers compared to other European presidents. The presidential elections are held every six years. He or she determines the country's foreign policy, acts as supreme chief of the defensive forces and appoints the highest governmental officials, all military officers as well as the government itself, which must also win the confidence of the parliament.

At times, the interaction among the parties has been so difficult that the result has often led to short-lived and weak minority governments. It has been said that

our times are devoid of ideals. Political nuances have decreased to such an extent that nowadays it's not uncommon to form a government on a majority coalition for its entire term of office.

Citizens seek justice in independent courts. Their independence is guaranteed by the fact that judges virtually cannot be dismissed. The Council of State's Chancellor of Justice is not only a general prosecutor but also the highest supervising officer of law with extensive powers for administrating it. For his part, the Parliamentary Ombudsman also takes good care of legal protection of citizens. Anyone is entitled to turn to him with his or her woes.

Finns find themselves at school for practically all their childhood and youth, and even beyond. In daycare centres, teachers and assistants strive to provide a good and balanced future for the children. Six-year-olds often go to pre-school and the lower level of comprehensive school starts at the age of seven. Comprehensive school lasts for nine years. At the age of sixteen students complete their compulsory education and can continue either in vocational education or in upper secondary school. Nearly all schools, apart from a few special schools, are communal. Instruction is free.

Many continue their studies after school and pursue

academic disciplines, in the country's twenty or more universities. Finland is proud of its long academic tradition. The first university was founded in Turku in 1640.

It's not easy for a student to get into university. After

the matriculation exams and weeks or months of training for entrance exams, the doors to universities eventually only open their doors to two out of every five applicants. In the most coveted areas the ratio is as low as three out of a hundred.

National defence in Finland is based on demographic and geographical reality – and on harsh experience. Finns have always had to think that they have to defend themselves against the enemy alone, with their

own weapons and without anyone else's help. Throughout the years the defense forces have become part of society itself. This is evident in Finland's compulsory military service for men and, above all, in the willingness of citizens to defend themselves. They also trust in their ability to do just that.

Nowadays, when Finns are asked for a typical Finnish characteristic they usually mention the desire to defend their country, first. Among all institutions the defense forces are valued the highest, even more than the President, the parliament, the church or the judicial system. Behind this phenomenon there would seem to be not only nationalistic tendencies but also the spectre of international insecurity.

The majority of men still choose military service. Only about seven per cent of the age group eligible for national service opt for the civilian alternative.

Since 1995 women, too, have been able to do military service voluntarily. Even before that women were allowed to take part in national defence work within the constraints of various volunteer organizations.

For a long time Finland had the questionable honour of having the smallest percentage of foreigner inhabitants in Europe. This protracted isolation has had its effects: seven out of every ten Finns see fear or hatred of foreigners as a Finnish characteristic. Such attitudes can even be seen in practice.

Although the amount of foreigners arriving is Finland is insignificant by international standards, the number of permanent foreign citizens living in the country since the beginning of the 1990s has trebled. And this, combined with the fact that our foreign population has also settled outside cities in the countryside, has certainly made foreigners more noticeable everywhere.

In 1994, one in every four foreigners held a Swedish passport, a few years later one in ten. The largest immigration to Finland has been from the ex-Soviet Union, especially from Russia and Estonia.

There are considerably more Finns living abroad than there are foreigners living in Finland: altogether, including third and fourth generations, there are some 1.2 million Finnish expatriates scattered all over the globe.

Finland's swamps were formed from the biomass that sank to the bottom of the lakes during the last glacial period. Ice, several kilometres thick, had gouged a giant indentation in the earth's crust which then started to rise after the ice had melted. Consequentially, the lakes dried up and the sediments remained as swamps.

This 10,000 year-old biological museum is being depleted within the course of one generation. The swamp also provides a luscious landscape.

The burning-over of woodland is an old Finnish way of preparing land for cultivation. The cleared and burnt forest feeds the land with nutrients while ridding it of insect pests and weeds. By implementing crop rotation the burn-beaten land then provides several harvests, even without fertilization.

The eastern gate of Lake Saimaa
is lush Lappeenranta, home
to 35,000 people and the centre
of Southern Karelia.
The old lake steamer, Taimi III,
is easy to spot in the town's
nostalgic passenger harbour.
From Lappeenranta you can take
a cruise to the Saimaa archipelago,
to Savonlinna and on through
the Saimaa Canal to
Vyborg in Russia.

Imatra power plant is the largest of its kind in Finland. Vuoksi, which once flowed free in a rocky channel, was Finland's modest answer to Niagara falls. This beautiful craggy channel produced a breathtaking but lethal rapids.

People at the marketplace can babble almost as fast as the rapids.

Olavinlinna was founded in 1475
on the undefined border between
Finland (under Sweden) and
Russia to protect the Finnish
population from Russian attack.
A trading centre soon sprung
up around the castle.
Savonlinna was granted a town
charter by Pietari Brahe in 1639.
Before the exact border was
settled on there were countless
battles around the castle for
a few hundred years.
Nowadays the only fighting
that takes place there is on stage in
the castle's inner court – and in
strict accordance with the libretto.
The Savonlinna Opera Festival
was launched in 1968 and since
then has taken place every year
in July.

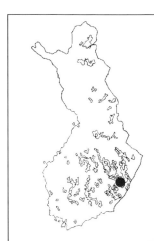

Ilomantsi, east of St. Petersburg, is
Finland's easternmost municipality.
It's the meeting place for the Eastern
and Western churches and culture.
The priest, Henrik Renqvist (1789-1866),
was an adamant opponent of alcohol.
He published 66 books in his lifetime;
a record in its time; and not a bad
achievement even by today's
standards.

Henrik Renqvist's birthplace in Kirvesvaara,
in Ilomantsi, is still inhabited by the family.
The house also functions as a museum.

In contrast to the pietist severity of the Renqvistians, Ilomantsi also enjoys a rich Orthodox tradition celebrated in village festivals. They're usually held in memory of a local patron saint. The most famous of these is the Ilja village festival, celebrated in commemoration of the prophet Elijah, in July.

Starting from a sanctuary, it features the Procession of the Cross, the sanctification of water and a visit to the cemetery.

Karelia's frontier
landscape is
a combination of
ridges, swamps, hills,
lakes and ponds.
Here we see a view of
Lake Ilomantsi.
On the shores the
towers of the Orthodox
Church outmatch the
treetops. 19% of
Ilomantsi's inhabitants
are members of
the Orthodox
Church.

Culture and religion don't always obey borders. Since the time of Russian rule a strong Orthodox tradition has thrived in Finland's eastern frontier. The Russian part of Karelia, however, has already lost much of its verve for the religion.

A priest from St. Petersburg visiting the Sonkaranta church in Ilomantsi. Time for quiet meditation in nature's place of worship.

Young devotees guarantee an ongoing tradition.

When Mother
Nature settles
down for her
winter rest
she takes on
a decisively
different beauty.
A summer
thicket becomes
a snowy garden;
more than
enough to slow
down the sprint
of the hare.

Finland's
long period
of darkness
may depress,
but it's good
to remember
that seasonal
change is
a richness;
it gives
time
a rhythm.

The Finnish summer can be
described as having two
daytimes back-to-back.
Likewise, its winter has two
concurrent nighttimes.
But if the sun is allowed to fall
upon Finland's bitterly beautiful
wintery landscape even for a
moment, it will capture
the heart of many
a tourist.

Tar, the black gold of
Finland's forests,
gave birth to Oulu.
Even 500 years ago the
Swedes and Russians
were fighting for control
of the area.
Above right:
in the foreground,
we can see Oulu's seashore
town theater.

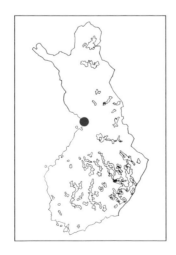

Autumn marketplace tables buckle under
the gold of the swamps; cloudberries.

Top: The town centre still features
several Empire-, wooden and
Art Nouveau-style buildings.
Above: the towns's highest point;
the church, renovated after fire
according to Engel's designs.

Modern Oulu's ace card is high-tech.
Polar Oy manufactures pulsimeters.

103

The estuary of Kemi, Finland's largest river,
has lured salmon catchers for 4,000 years.
The Senate granted Kemi a town
charter in 1869.
Today, Kemi is a thriving industrial
area and cultural centre.
The town centre is dominated
by a 58-metre-tall town hall.
German attempts to blow it up during
the war caused it to sway for many years.
This was not surprising, considering
it only had one wall effectively supporting
it and the four bottom floors were missing.
The history of all the world's gemstones
can be found in the harbour's
precious stone gallery.

Kemi's large wood processing plants are located in Veitsiluoto and in Karihaara, the latter lying on the mouth of the River Kemi. Both employ mechanical and chemical wood processing. The raw wood for these giant plants is transported by road from a large area of Southern Lapland: log floating ceased long ago. Ajos's deep-water harbour dispatches the manufactured products all over the world.

On the 16th of June, 1959,
a diver called Matti Matilainen
found a stone, northeast of Kemi,
containing chrome oxide.
The discovery lead to the
foundation of a mine in 1964.
Within four years its production
had grown to its present size.
Although the ore body is poor
by international standards, the
mine is so large that it can be
quarried for at least 200 years.
The mineral is dressed in the mine
area, and the manufactured metal
released from Outokumpu's
refined steel mill in Tornio.

The largest of the few rivers
that haven't been harnessed to
the power economy is
the River Tornio.
Tornio's Kukkola rapids are
unrivalled.
For ages its salmon
have been caught by netting
and the catch shared among
the salmon farms in the area.
You can taste glow-fried
whitefish in the storehouse
by the riverbank.

Swedish-Finnish marriages,
comprising partners from
both sides of the Tornio river
valley, are popular.
The ferryman statue is
a reminder of times past.

Aavasaksa – one of Mountain Lapland's oldest
tourist attractions.

Arktikum, built on the banks of the River Ounas, is a unique exhibition and research centre. It has been compared with a cluster of Lapland amethyst.

Until the end of 1870s the little village of Rovaniemi sat anonymously in the confluence of the River Ounas and the River Kemi.

Then, in 1881, the big logging sites arrived, and with it the famous Rovaniemi market which attracted settlers from the area.

Lapland's new centre enjoyed uninterrupted growth even when the market town was completely destroyed in the immediate aftermath of the Second World War.

The town hosts a wide variety of events throughout the year. Attractions bring the town half a million tourists each year. The puukko-knife is an all-round tool and much-valued souvenir.

Skates and skis
and
Flying Finns

The Finns are a sporty nation – they're avid and active sports enthusiasts. It's often said that Finns have run themselves onto the world map. This cliché is undoubtedly true.

Finland's success in sports has had a tremendous impact on raising national self-esteem. In those heady years of 'Olympic ecstasy' in the 20s and 30s, Finland was clearly one of the leading sports countries in the world. The uncrowned king of runners was Paavo Nurmi, the Flying Finn. Athletes, wrestlers, skaters and skiers have put the most medals around their necks, but marksmen and gymnasts have also brought distinction to the country.

After the Second World War Finns felt disappointed when they didn't achieve the same level of success as they had previously. The 1952 Olympic Games, held in Helsinki, brought some consolation, however. Hosting the biggest sporting event of its time and carrying it off successfully was just the thing to raise people's spirits. After all, the republic was only just recovering from paying its war reparations – ahead of time.

Over the decades Finland has quite definitely maintained its position alongside the giant sporting nations. In addition to competitive sports, increasing attention has also been paid to fitness training. In the 1960s, several national organizations were founded in order to help its promotion. Hundreds of thousands of people were drawn into all kinds of fitness training events and physical exercise such as jogging, running, etc.

The most culturally indicative of all Finnish sports has always been cross-country skiing. Children learn to ski shortly after they've learnt to walk, and often continue skiing throughout their lives. Nowadays, teenagers are more into down-hill skiing and snow-boarding. Large-scale winter sports resorts have been set up all over the country for this very purpose.

A relatively recent success story is ice hockey. Finland's success at winning the 1995 world ice

hockey championships sent the whole country into a spin. And such enthusiasm is not only confined to the international arena. Finnish ice hockey league games during the winter season fill up large ice halls with thousands of sports fans. Water is also a favourite element for some Finns. Week in, week out, Finnish swimmers have achieved considerable international success. The sports itself, though, has yet to attract the interest of a wider public.

In Finland, the number of sports fans far exceeds the number of people who actually go in for sports themselves. Competitive sporting events are followed by hundreds of thousands of people in Finland. When you add the amount of spectators sat in front of the television or listening to the radio, the unofficial attendance can sometimes rise to a couple of million.

In terms of Olympic gold medals and world champions Finland's hall-of-fame heroes and heroines are,

Paavo Nurmi´s statue at
Helsinki´s Olympic Stadium.

112

PAAVO
NURMI

n addition to the legendary Paavo Nurmi, the runners, Hannes Kolehmainen, Ville Ritola and Lasse Viren, the skater, Clas Thunberg, the skiers, Veikko Hakulinen, Eero Mäntyranta and Marja-Liisa Kirvesniemi, the ski-jumper, Matti Nykänen and the rower, Pertti Karppinen. Everybody has heard of Finnish rally and racing-car drivers, the most famous of whom are world champion rally drivers and the 1982 Formula One winner, Keke Rosberg.

Although Finns are delighted with their claim to international fame in the field of sport, there are no international competitions for Finland's national sport, Finnish baseball. This game, developed at the beginning of the century from the traditional 'king ball' and American baseball, boasts tens of thousands of enthusiastic players and half a million or so regular summer spectators. The climax of the season is the annual East against West game.

The point where the waters of the River Kemi widen to form a lake has always been a good spot for settlements.

Nowadays the area is known as Kemijärvi, Finland's northernmost town.

The timeless backwoods village of Mutenia was originally built on the banks of a measly little river. But when Lokka reservoir, Finland's first artificial lake and the largest in Europe, was completed, the old village stayed put. Some of the houses belong to Kemijoki Ltd, the owner of the reservoir.

A song says that Lake Inari is
as deep as it is long.
It's certainly long enough
to provide a runway for
light airplanes.
In addition to sightseeing
flights the planes are also used
for flying prospectors and their
gear to gold areas.
The planes can land near
their claims thanks to a runway
built in the uplands.
The River Inari is one
of the border rivers between
Finland and Norway.
Its most appealing sight is
probably the Inari falls.

Inset: the chamber in
the Mutenia village museum.
President Urho Kekkonen
slept there.

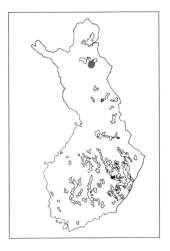

A Lapp museum was built by
the mouth of the River Juutua,
near Inari village.

It depicts the Inari and Utsjoki
Lapp areas' sources of livelihood,
ways of life and everyday artefacts.

Practically all of the River Lemmenjoki's shores and streams have been claimed for gold washing.

The tree limit cuts across the
Jäkäläpää area.

Here, gold can be found several
metres below ground level .

Turf dwellings have been used by several generations.
The flat dome of Jäkäläpää has

an airfield and telephone.
Gems, too, can be found by panning the sand.

The River Teno (Teädnu or Deatnu in the Lapp language), which separates the Lapps of Finland from the Lapps of Norway, cuts across contrasting landscapes: below it's still green, despite the first signs of autumn; above lies snow.

Raja-Jooseppi's reindeer round-up run by the
Vuotso Reindeer Owners' Association.

Reindeer management is the most important source of livelihood for Lapps, or Samis; the European Union's only indigenious people. In addition to its meat, the reindeer's skin and horns are also used for clothes and ornaments.
Reindeer milk is exceptionally nutritious, thanks to its high fat content. Reindeer round-ups are held in early winter. At this time, the fawns are marked with their owners' earmarks. Reindeer destined for slaughter or for use as draught reindeer, as well as extra bucks are all caught by lasso.

Draught reindeer are harnessed to help market Father Christmas and exotic Lapland.

Many countries, including Norway and Greenland, claim to be the home of Santa Claus, but the truth is that he comes from Korvatunturi, in Finnish Lapland. Nowadays, however, he tends to be rather sophisticated, directing operations from his headquarters in Rovaniemi.

Semi-tame reindeer are an integral part of Lapland.
Nowadays they are also an essential component
of tourism.

The top names in Finnish design can all be found along the Esplanadis and in Unioninkatu, within easy reach of Helsinki's passenger harbours.

The hallmark of many esteemed artists can be found
in their works; sometimes, works are inspired by
archeological finds or popular fairytale characters.

The input of female artists in Finnish design is particularly evident. Some of the most well-known works include Armi Ratia's Marimekko clothes and decorative ornaments, Kaija Aarikka's jewellery and wooden items, Anu Pentik's leather goods and ceramics, and Artek's wooden furniture.

Design Forum Finland's exhibition space is also located in Esplanadi. Its exhibitions cover the very latest in Finnish design, covering everything from jewellery to trucks.

Furs are in great demand in Finland's northern climate. Their development has also brought fantastic results, ranging from classical solutions to striking designs.

Finnish shoppers are continuously lured by friendly pedestrian streets with terrace cafés and splendid shopping centres. On the right, the Forum shopping complex in Helsinki, opened in 1986.

Alvar Aalto's humane functionalism certainly left its mark in the Finnish way of living. Its characteristics are a sensible division of space, and elegance combined with simplicity, comfortability and cosiness.

As can be seen, pets are very popular even in towns – yet another indication of Finns' longing for nature.

The most common denominators
in the way Finns use their
sparetime can be found in
nature and sports.
The advent of summer finds
Finns moving towards the waters,
where they can enjoy a sauna,
go swimming, row their boats
or go fishing.
Sports can be enjoyed alone or
in groups, relaxing on a bench
or straining with a club or bat.
Summer is also a time for
listening to the Word of God,
either as a family or at numerous
religious gatherings.

Winter's ice and snow
offer many opportunities
for both spectators and active
sportsmen and -women: you
can ski, skate, go downhill
skiing or tobogganing.
Finland's striking seasonal
variations are also a delight
for fishermen.
Ice angling is the focal
point of many a wintery
Sunday, regardless of
the catch.

Evening at Lake Kemi.

A journey into silence

Finland's most enticing tourist attraction is nature herself. Specifically, its archipelago, forests and lakes. Compared to the densely-populated areas of Central Europe, Finland offers a breathtakingly beautiful, clean and untouched natural environment.

The majority of the jobs relating to tourism are situated in Southern Finland. The most famous destination is, however, Lapland. Its endless hilly plains can accommodate even the largest tourist groups. Lapland's lure lies in its stunning scenery, serene silence and sun-filled summer nights. It's also a much-favoured location in the autumn. The forests glow with autumnal hues and nature enwraps herself in a kaleidoscope of yellow, red and brown. In the winter, Lapland's mountains are irresistible to even the most reluctant skier. And there's a very real chance that you'll bear witness to one of the most spectacular displays nature can offer: the aurora borealis.

Finland's most famous inhabitant, Santa Claus, who resides at the Arctic Circle, has a very special international charm. The correspondence generated by him and his Christmas helpers is impressive, as is his touristic pull for Lapland. The south also offers all kinds

of theme parks. Some find them attractive, others don't.

The cultured traveller should not expect to come across many surprises in Finland. But the summertime does offer a feast of festivals. There are hundreds of theatrical, operatic and dance events, chamber music festivals, symphony concerts, as well as pop and jazz events. And it's not unusual to find world-famous artists performing

amidst the most idyllic of summer settings. Grand and modest summer events are organized all over the country.

Excellent travel connections create a good framework for tourism. There are some 6,000 kilometres of railway and an endless array of railway coaches. Bus connections are impressive, even by international standards: bus or coach routes cover around 80 per cent of Finland's 76,000 kilometre-long road network, with 40,000 daily scheduled departures. Finnair and its subsidiaries fly regularly to 25 domestic airports.

Accommodation is abundant and the hotels are modern, excellently furnished and well-fitted. Finland has around 350 camping sites and 160 youth hostels. Economical summer

hotels can also be found in university towns. As soon as the tourist season is over they function once again as student accommodation.

Working Finns are on holiday for approximately one month in the summer and for a week in the winter. This usually coincides with children's holidays. Many Finns spend much of their holiday and many weekends at summer cottages. In several countryside locations the number of inhabitants can increase manyfold

during the summer holiday season. There are around 400,000 summer cottages altogether in Finland which house some 800,000 summer inhabitants.

Finns spend a total of ten million nights in Finnish hotels, on camping sites and in other accommodation. This means roughly two nights per inhabitant. Foreign tourists spend approximately four million nights in Finland. There's still room for improvement in the tourist trade, since at the beginning of 1990s only four out of every ten of Finland's hotel rooms were in use. Six out of ten were, even by Finnish standards, needlessly silent.

But there again – there's a lot of room in Finland.